ideals
FRIENDSHIP

Vol. 50, No. 6

Publisher, Patricia A. Pingry
Editor, Tim Hamling
Art Director, Patrick McRae
Contributing Editors, Lansing Christman, Deana Deck, Russ Flint, Pamela Kennedy, Heidi King, Nancy Skarmeas
Editorial Assistant, Laura Matter

ISBN 0-8249-1111-3

IDEALS—Vol. 50, No. 6 September MCMXCIII IDEALS (ISSN 0019-137X) is published eight times a year: February, March, May, June, August, September, November, December by IDEALS PUBLISHING CORPORATION, 565 Marriott Drive, Nashville, TN 37214. Second-class postage paid at Nashville, Tennessee and additional mailing offices. Copyright © MCMXCIII by IDEALS PUBLISHING CORPORATION. POSTMASTER: Send address changes to Ideals, PO Box 148000, Nashville, TN 37214-8000. All rights reserved. Title IDEALS registered U.S. Patent Office.

SINGLE ISSUE—$4.95
ONE-YEAR SUBSCRIPTION—eight consecutive issues as published—$19.95
TWO-YEAR SUBSCRIPTION—sixteen consecutive issues as published—$35.95
Outside U.S.A., add $6.00 per subscription year for postage and handling.

ACKNOWLEDGMENTS

OLD APPLE HOUSE IN AUTUMN excerpted from *APPLES OF GOLD* by Grace Noll Crowell. Copyright © 1950 by Grace Noll Crowell. Reprinted by arrangement with Harper San Francisco, a division of HarperCollins Publishers Inc. A LEAF-TREADER from *THE POETRY OF ROBERT FROST* edited by Edward Connery Lathem. Copyright 1936 by Robert Frost, © 1964 by Lesley Frost Ballantine, © 1969 by Henry Holt and Company, Inc. Reprinted by permission of Henry Holt and Company, Inc. FIRST NAME FRIENDS by Edgar A. Guest from *THE PATH TO HOME*, copyright ©1919 by The Reilly & Lee Co. Used by permission of the author's estate. AUTUMN MOOD from *OVER THE RIDGE* by Patience Strong. Copyright 1943 by Patience Strong. Reprinted by permission of Rupert Crew Limited. Our Sincere Thanks to the following authors whom we were unable to contact: Mary Jeannette Bassett for UNTIL; Abbie Farwell Brown for FRIENDS; Elsie M. Farr for FRIENDS THROUGH CORRESPONDENCE; Marion Rollins Guptill for WHAT IS THE WORTH OF A FRIEND?; Florence M. Hurst for TRULY FRIENDS; and Bertye Young Williams for THE FRIEND WHO JUST STANDS BY.

Four-color separations by Rayson Films, Inc., Waukesha, Wisconsin.

Printing by The Banta Company, Menasha, Wisconsin. Printed on Weyerhauser Husky.

The paper used in this publication meets the minimum requirements of American National Standard for Information Sciences—Permanence of Paper for Printed Library Materials, ANSI Z39.48-1984.

Unsolicited manuscripts will not be returned without a self-addressed stamped envelope.

Inside Front Cover
George Hinke

Inside Back Cover
Richard Hook

Cover Photo
Ralph Luedtke

Goldenrod, Gold Goldenrod

Loise Pinkerton Fritz

O goldenrod, gold goldenrod,
You fill September's fields;
With August's heyday in the past,
You follow on its heels.
On wand-like stems you flaunt your gold;
A scenic sight you are.
O goldenrod, gold goldenrod,
Your beauty reaches far.

O goldenrod, gold goldenrod,
Coarse bloom with stems so tall,
Your splendid yellow flowerets
Are fashioned for the fall.
For when the summer flowers depart
From summer's floral fest,
O goldenrod, gold goldenrod,
You're there at fall's behest.

Photo Opposite
ASTERS AND GOLDENROD
Moosehorn National Wildlife Refuge, Maine
William Johnson
Johnson's Photography

2

Farewell to Summer

Elisabeth Weaver Winstead

A message in the dry, crisp air
Stirs each sight and sound;
The crickets croon a steady tune
As rustling leaves drift down.

Now all the singing swallows
From woods and meadows go;
In dales and shaded hollows
Damp, billowing breezes blow.

The blossoms of gleaming asters
Show yellow, bronze, and red,
Where yesterday grew a profusion
Of crimson dahlias instead.

We bid good-bye to sweet summer,
Fresh fragrance of new-mown hay,
Knowing treasured summer soon
Will silently tiptoe away.

Farewell to green-grassed summer,
Rich storehouse of life and birth,
Shining splendors of countryside,
Warm rhapsody of earth.

ASHUELOT COVERED BRIDGE
Ashuelot, New Hampshire
William Johnson
Johnson's Photography

September

Helen Hunt Jackson

The goldenrod is yellow;
The corn is turning brown;
The trees in apple orchards
With fruit are bending down.

The gentian's bluest fringes
Are curling in the sun;
In dusty pods the milkweed
Its hidden silk has spun.

The sedges flaunt their harvest
In every meadow nook,
And asters by the brookside
Make asters in the brook.

From dewy lanes at morning,
The grapes' sweet odors rise;
At noon the roads all flutter
With yellow butterflies.

By all these lovely tokens,
September days are here
With summer's best of weather
And autumn's best of cheer.

But none of all this beauty
Which floods the earth and air
Is unto me the secret
Which makes September fair.

'Tis a thing which I remember;
To name it thrills me yet—
One day of one September
I never can forget.

Autumn

Dawn Zapletal

Did maples blaze this red
in seasons past,
And skies look quite as deeply
blue and vast?

Were the pumpkins as plump and
orange as now?
Did apples hang as heavy
on the bough?

Did purple grapes bend down
the burdened vine
With promise of a robust
winter wine?

Why does the fall that makes
some people sad
Make me feel joyously
fulfilled and glad?

Yet even I may shed
a tender tear
In fond farewell to yet
another year.

Photo Opposite
CHANGING SEASONS
Candor, New York
Ed Cooper Photography

Photo Overleaf
AUTUMN REFLECTION
Horseshoe Lake Conservation Area
Alexander County, Illinois
Michael Shedlock Photography

The Basket of Harvest

Loise Pinkerton Fritz

The basket of harvest is long and it's wide;
It's woven with birdsong and bright butterflies.

The basket of harvest is fragrantly filled
With scents of wildflowers God planted at will.

The basket of harvest is laden with fruit,
With grains and plump berries for me and for you.

I thank God for giving this gift of great worth,
The basket of harvest, the fields of the earth.

Photo Opposite
COTTONSTONE FARM STAND
Orford, New Hampshire
William Johnson
Johnson's Photography

13

FROM MY
G·A·R·D·E·N
JOURNAL

Deana Deck

FRESH SPEARMINT, Grant Heilman Photography.

The Refreshing Variety of Mint

When I was a child, one of my favorite ways to cool off on a warm day was to lie down in my grandma's mint bed, chew on a stem, and count clouds for awhile. I would astonish and amaze my friends who doubted my ability to "eat leaves" as I nibbled a sprig from the plants. It made me smell terrific and gave me a fresh burst of energy.

I also used to treat my friends to mint julep colas. I'd put some ice cubes and mint leaves in a tea towel, smash them with a hammer, drop the crushed ice and leaves into a tall glass, and add the cola. Although my mother wasn't too happy about the minty stains on her good tea towels, my friends were suitably impressed; and I found a treat I enjoy to this day, although now I'm more likely to use iced tea than cola, and I no

longer take a hammer to the mint.

I do take shears to the mint, however, and because it is one of the more versatile plants in the garden, I find myself constantly clipping stems for one purpose or another. You may be surprised to learn how many plants are in the mint family. In addition to the familiar peppermint and spearmint, the vast family includes thyme, lavender, sage, rosemary, catnip, and lemon balm.

Mint can be grown from seeds, but if you already have a plant or know someone who does, an easier method of propagation is simply to root a few stems in water. Otherwise, seeds can be ordered from nearly any garden catalog.

Mint is very easy to grow, either in the garden or in containers on balconies or patios. In the garden, it grows best in partial shade and

14

moderately rich soil kept slightly moist, so I always grow it against the house in the vicinity of the water spigots. A few leaves may be crushed every time you use the hose, but such damage adds a delightfully fresh fragrance to the air.

Mint does tend to spread, but you can control this spreading by installing a root barrier of boards about six inches into the ground around the bed. Some gardeners avoid the problem by just planting the mint in pots buried in the soil.

Mint winters over well in most climates, but if you are growing it in containers on a balcony or patio in a cold climate, you should bring it indoors for winter so the roots don't freeze. If you can't move the plants indoors, cut some stems and grow them in water in a sunny window until spring.

If you prefer, mint can be easily dried for winter use. Cut the mint's long branches, fasten them with rubber bands, and hang them upside down in a dry, airy location until they are dry enough to crumble when touched. Store the dried mint in an airtight container.

Mint has a thousand uses, and almost as many faces. The most popular mints used in recipes are peppermint and spearmint, in either the standard or curly form, but there are other more exotic variations. For instance, there are a fruity apple mint and a sweet, purple-tinted candy mint; there are a variety favored for potpourri called *Eau de Cologne* and a variegated mint called *Emerald and Gold* that is very attractive in floral arrangements. If you want mint with a difference, try ginger mint, grapefruit mint, lavender mint, orange mint, or pineapple mint. There's even a chocolate mint!

If you like roasted lamb, you know that it is always enhanced by a generous dollop of spearmint jelly. This jelly is easy to make. Use a basic apple jelly recipe and, after boiling the apple juice, simply pour a cup of it over one-half cup of chopped mint and let the mixture stand for twenty minutes. Then strain and proceed with the recipe's directions.

Mint can be used to make a caffeine-free tea that wonderfully alleviates the symptoms of a head cold. It can also be added to regular tea for additional flavor. To make mint tea, pour a cup of boiling water over a teaspoon or tea ball full of fresh or dried mint leaves. Tea brewed in this fashion makes a much more flavorful iced tea than a glass of plain tea simply garnished with a sprig of mint.

Use the same technique with pennyroyal leaves to make a flea-repellent spray for your pets. Pour a quart of hot water over one-half cup of fresh pennyroyal leaves and steep until cool; then strain. Spray the animal lightly, without soaking the coat, and do not give internally, as pennyroyal is for external use only, even for humans!

An additional cold-symptom reliever is mint steam. Make an infusion by adding a handful of peppermint or spearmint leaves (half that amount if they are dried) to about four quarts of water and bring to a boil. Remove from the heat and place your face under a large towel and over the open pot. Be careful not to get too close to the steam to avoid being scalded. You don't need to have a cold or congested sinuses to benefit from this treatment. A mint facial sauna using the same technique does wonders for the complexion as well as the spirit.

You can make mint shampoo by adding a strong infusion of mint to commercial castile shampoo available from organic food stores. When placed in ornamental bottles, mint shampoo makes an attractive gift.

For a fragrant, cooling mint bath, add a cup of fresh mint leaves to a quart of boiling water. Remove the mint from the heat and steep for twenty minutes, and then strain and pour into a tub of warm water.

Placing mint in vases throughout the house creates a living potpourri, keeps the air smelling fresh and clean, and provides more rooted cuttings than you'll be able to use. Adding a generous cutting of fresh mint sprigs to an arrangement of white carnations and baby's breath makes a wonderful, inexpensive centerpiece for the kitchen table. With its numerous uses, mint will soon become one of your most valuable plants in the garden.

Deana Deck lives in Nashville, Tennessee, where her garden column is a regular feature in The Tennessean.

Autumn Mood

Patience Strong

I love the earth in autumn mood,
    The misty dawns, the golden noon.
I love the quiet evening hour,
    The glory of the harvest moon.
I love the last slow-fading rose
    That lingers on the garden wall,
The mellow sun that seems to shed
    The light of blessing over all,

Old houses wrapped in crimson cloaks,
    The stain of creepers on grey stone,
Woods of russet, bronze, and scarlet,
    Leaves of every tint and tone,
Season of the golden hours
    With winter nigh and summer past,
Nature in her brightest garments,
    Clothed in beauty to the last.

May the final phase of life
    Be like the earth in autumn mood,
Rich with blessing and contentment,
    Full of peace and quietude.
For God's mercies glad and grateful,
    Having neither doubts nor fears,
May I walk with my beloved
    In the autumn of the years.

AUTUMN BRILLIANCE
West Woodstock, Vermont
Laatsch-Hupp Photography

CHRONICLE
Country
Lansing Christman

There's a lot of summer left in September. The month is a meeting of the old and new, initiating the change from summer and pointing the way to fall.

Summer has played its role as the season of maturity; now it is up to September to chart the course to autumn and beyond. The change is already under way. Notice the shorter hours of sunlight and the longer hours of moonlight and shining stars.

The outdoor world is showing vivid evidence as sumac leaves don their autumn garb of scarlet. The dogwood leaves have taken on their striking colors, and once their leaves fall, the bright red berries become far more spectacular. The woodbine climbing walls and trees and fencerows becomes a deep red, and the lemon-colored blooms of witch hazel on the pasture ledge are starting their parade of beauty. There are still wildflowers along the byways; goldenrod

with its spires of blooms point to the sky.

At higher elevations, leaves are beginning to turn red, scarlet, gold, bronze, and maroon. The foliage festival will soon creep down the mountainsides to our own woodlands and door-yards here at the foot of the Blue Ridge Mountains.

Not only are there colors of dazzling shades, but there are birdsongs too. The warble of the bluebird is just as sweet as it was in March, and the song sparrow's melody is just as tender and sweet as ever. When I hear the robin's carol, the birds bickering in the wild grape thickets, and the tremolo of the chipmunks and the chattering of the squirrels, I think of God's plan in the year's recessional.

Each autumn day that brings us a blossom or a highly-colored leaf is a day of beauty and loveliness. Each autumn day that brings us a song will be a day of cheer. All go toward nourishing the heart with promise and hope, for hope springs eternal from the heart and dreams of man.

The author of two published books, Lansing Christman has been contributing to Ideals *for over twenty years. Mr. Christman has also been published in several American, foreign, and braille anthologies. He lives in rural South Carolina.*

Then Autumn

Garnett Ann Schultz

There are no words to quite express the beauty of the fall;
No poet's pen or artist's brush can ever capture all
The flaming red, the wondrous gold, the tender bit of green,
The garden path ablaze and bright with autumn's changing scene.

There is no way one can describe where scarlet sage abounds,
The humblest field, an ecstasy where goldenrod is found
Across the ever waiting hills adorned in nature's robe,
The purple splendor of the fall, where none but God shall probe.

There are no words for autumn days; our eyes alone must see,
And never can we capture all her crimson certainties.
The flaming hills and changing trees majestically shall stand,
For autumn's world is proud and still, a world of beauty grand.

There is no one, however great, can ever find it all,
From browning grass to bending sky, dear Mother Nature's fall.
And she alone shall take her brush, yet there shall be no sound,
As summer changeth quietly and autumn doth come round.

Photo Opposite
AUTUMN LANDSCAPE
Near Epoufette, Michigan
Ed Cooper Photography

Thoughts on Autumn

Nathaniel Hawthorne

Still later in the season, Nature's tenderness waxes stronger. It is impossible not to be fond of our Mother now; for She is so fond of us! At other periods, She does not make this impression on me, or only at rare intervals; but in these genial days of autumn, when She has perfected her harvests and accomplished every needful thing that was given Her to do, then She over-

flows with a blessed superfluity of love. She has leisure to caress Her children now. It is good to be alive at such times. Thank heaven for breath—yes, for mere breath—when it is made up of a heavenly breeze like this! It comes with a real kiss upon our cheeks; it would linger fondly around us if it might; but since it must be gone, it embraces us with its whole kindly heart and passes onward to embrace likewise the next thing that it meets. A blessing is flung abroad and scattered far and wide over the earth, to be gathered up by all who choose. I recline upon the still unwithered grass and whisper to myself, "O perfect day! O beautiful world! O beneficent God!" And it is the promise of a blessed eternity; for our Creator would never have made such lovely days and have given us the deep hearts to enjoy them, above and beyond all thought, unless we were meant to be immortal. This sunshine is the golden pledge thereof. It beams through the gates of paradise and shows us glimpses far inward.

The Ripened Leaves

Margaret E. Sangster

Said the leaves upon the branches
One sunny autumn day,
"We've finished all our work, and now
We can no longer stay.

So our gowns of red and yellow
And our cloaks of sober brown
Must be worn before the frost comes
And we go rustling down.

We've had a jolly summer
With the birds that built their nests

24

Beneath our green umbrellas and
The squirrels that were our guests.

But we cannot wait for winter,
And we do not care for snow;
When we hear the wild northwesters,
We loose our clasp and go.

But we hold our heads up bravely
Unto the very last
And shine in pomp and splendor as
Away we flutter fast.

In the mellow autumn noontide,
We kiss and say good-bye,
And through the naked branches then
May children see the sky."

Readers' Reflections

Editor's Note: Readers are invited to submit unpublished, original poetry for possible publication in future issues of *Ideals*. Please send copies only; manuscripts will not be returned. Writers receive $10 for each published submission. Send material to "Readers' Reflections," Ideals Publishing Corporation, P.O. Box 140300, Nashville, TN 37214-0300.

Autumn Benediction

A tangy, smoky fragrance fills the air.
Autumn paints her colors everywhere.

A landscape of russets, reds, and golds,
This masterpiece of God unfolds.

High overhead the birds are all in flight.
The harvest moon appears in the stillness of the night.

The frosted mist of twilight drifting over all
Is the silent benediction God sends us to recall.

Eleanor Joan Kearney
Shoreham, New York

26

Diamonds

Ever sacred is our friendship;
    There's nothing to pretend.
The greatest diamond on this earth
    Is the kindness of a friend!

Cherished are our faithful friends,
    True diamonds in disguise,
Sincere, kind, compassionate,
    And laughter in their eyes!

These close, endearing friendships
    Withstand the tests of time
And draw us closer year by year.
    Like diamonds, they're a prize.

A diamond is a precious stone,
    A truly treasured gem,
But this I treasure most of all,
    The handclasp of a friend!

Ardella Jones
Evansville, Indiana

Truly Friends

Countless are the reasons
We have to cherish friends—
For smiles when they're most needed,
For helping hands they lend,

For special confidences
They take the time to share,
For all the little loving ways
They show how much they care,

For their joy in our successes,
And their comfort in defeat.
For these and more, it's truly friends
Who make our lives complete.

Florence Hurst
Wallingford, Connecticut

Autumn Friend

June Masters Bacher

Our lives were new when first we met
And felt a friendship start,
And though the buds of youth have bloomed,
There's springtime in the heart.

For life must grow and life must change;
Else what's a summer for?
And now I find the years that bind
More precious than before.

For love that with each season grows
Can never know an end;
It reaches for eternity
Beside an autumn friend.

A Special Joy

June Masters Bacher

It's such a special joy to find
A friend who says, "Now I don't mind";
An it's-no-problem kind of friend
Who knows exactly what to lend;
A this-is-nothing piece of cheer
When you have had it up to here;

A let-me-help-you friend who'll say,
"Now you don't owe me for this day";
A friend who'll smile and hold your hand
And say, "Of course, I understand,"
And coax each frown into a smile.
God bless them; they make life worthwhile.

A Mile with Me

Henry van Dyke

O who will walk a mile with me
      Along life's merry way?
A comrade blithe and full of glee,
Who dares to laugh out loud and free
And let his frolic fancy play,
      Like a happy child
      Through the flowers gay
That fill the field and fringe the way
      Where he walks a mile with me.

And who will walk a mile with me
      Along life's weary way?
A friend whose heart has eyes to see
The stars shine out o'er darkening lea
And the quiet rest at the end o' the day;
      A friend who knows
      And dares to say
The brave, sweet words that cheer the way
      Where he walks a mile with me.

With such a comrade, such a friend,
I fain would walk till journey's end,
Through summer sunshine, winter rain,
And then? Farewell, we shall meet again!

BITS & PIECES

My only sketch, profile, of heaven is a large blue sky, and larger than the biggest I have seen in June—and in it are my friends—every one of them.

Emily Dickinson

I do not wish to treat friendships daintily, but with roughest courage. When they are real, they are not glass threads or frost-work, but the solidest thing we know.

Ralph Waldo Emerson

A friend should be one in whose understanding and virtue we can equally confide, and whose opinion we can value at once for its justness and its sincerity.

He who has made the acquisition of a judicious and sympathizing friend, may be said to have doubled his mental resources.

Robert Hall

By friendship you mean the greatest love, the greatest usefulness, the most open communication, the noblest sufferings, the severest truth, the heartiest counsel, and the greatest union of minds of which brave men and women are capable.

Jeremy Taylor

Be slow in choosing a friend, slower in changing.

Benjamin Franklin

Under the magnetism of friendship the modest man becomes bold; the shy, confident; the lazy, active; or the impetuous, prudent and peaceful.

William Makepeace Thackeray

The making of friends, who are real friends, is the best token we have of a man's success in life.

Edward Everett Hale

There is in friendship something of all relations, and something above them all. It is the golden thread that ties the heart of all the world.

John Evelyn

What Is the Worth of a Friend?

Marion Rollins Guptill

What is the worth of a friend?
If this were asked of me,
Warm thoughts of you would flood my heart,
And this my answer be—
A friend to me is many things;
No words express the worth
Of this rich gift that God bestows
To bless our walk on earth.

When disappointment's shadow falls
On special times I've planned,
A friend will make the sun shine through
With just "I understand."
Not like a flickering candlelight,
But a steady, glowing flame,
Knowing my failings and my faults
Yet loving me just the same.

Soothing the prick of life's sharp thorns
With nothing but a smile,
A friend is like Gibraltor's rock
In the lonely hour of trial,
Who does not stop with cheering words
But follows the words with deeds,
Not guilty of empty platitudes
For a soul burdened with needs.

A friend is one who weeps with me;
He pleads my grief in prayer
And sings with me in happiness
When good fortune is my share.
And so each time that we two meet,
Though often but minutes we spend,
I thank God for giving me
The blessing of such a friend.

GRANDMOTHER'S CREWELWORK PILLOW
Dianne Dietrich Leis, Photographer

The Friend Who Just Stands By

Bertye Young Williams

When trouble comes your soul to try,
You love the friend who just stands by.
Perhaps there's nothing he can do;
The thing is strictly up to you.

For there are troubles all your own
And paths the soul must tread alone,
Times when love can't smooth the road
Nor friendship lift the heavy load.

But just to know you have a friend
Who will stand by until the end,
Whose sympathy through all endures,
Whose warm handclasp is always yours—

It helps, someway, to pull you through,
Although there's nothing he can do.
And so with fervent heart you cry,
"God bless the friend who just stands by!"

FOR THE CHILDREN

ARTWORK BY RUSS FLINT

Friends

Abbie Farwell Brown

How good to lie a little while
And look up through the tree!
The sky is like a kind, big smile
Bent sweetly over me.

The sunshine flickers through the lace
Of leaves above my head
And kisses me upon the face
Like Mother before bed.

The wind comes stealing o'er the grass
To whisper pretty things,
And though I cannot see him pass,
I feel his careful wings.

So many gentle friends are near
Whom one can scarcely see;
A child should never feel a fear
Wherever he may be.

Phineas T. Barnum and James A. Bailey

The friendship between Phineas T. Barnum and James A. Bailey began with a business deal. In 1880, Barnum's decade old circus, "The Greatest Show on Earth," was thriving, so much so that its success spawned a group of small-er circuses, all with their eyes on Barnum's enthu-siastic audiences. The most successful of these was International Allied Shows, led by savvy thirty-three-year-old James A. Bailey. In a single year, Allied Shows completed a hugely profitable world tour and also became the first circus to use electricity under its tents. Audiences took notice, and so did Phineas T. Barnum. He approached Bailey and his partners with an offer too good to refuse. In 1881, the circuses joined forces, and a new, even greater, "Greatest Show on Earth" was born, soon to be known simply by the name "Barnum and Bailey's."

On the surface, Phineas Barnum and James Bailey had little in common. At the time of the merger, Barnum was seventy years old, a robust extrovert who thrived on publicity and set no limits on self-promotion. Barnum once said, "I don't care much what the papers say about me, provided they will say something." He saw to it that not a day went by when the papers didn't include mention of Phineas T. Barnum and his latest venture.

The much younger Bailey, on the other hand, shunned the spotlight, always declining his partner's persuasions to share the credit for their success. It was a well known fact that when celebrities visited the "Greatest Show on Earth"—and they frequently did, from U.S. President James A. Garfield to the Queen of England—Mr. Barnum would always be available, but Mr. Bailey would conveniently find a way to disappear.

Different as they were, Barnum and Bailey were a team unlike any other in the history of American entertainment. Barnum had the vision, the imagination, and the pure aplomb to continually amaze, excite, and entertain his audiences; and Bailey had the organizational and managerial skills to make it all possible. Barnum went to outrageous lengths to make his circus unlike any other. He talked the Royal Zoological Society of London out of one of their prized possessions, Jumbo the African elephant. Jumbo became a sensation in his new homeland while the English lamented his departure and wondered how the brash American had managed to take him away.

Barnum also made a hero of a dwarf named Charles Stratton, who under the name of General Tom Thumb captured the hearts of millions of Americans. Barnum's flair for the outra-geous was a lifelong trait. His entrance into show business began as the manager and promoter of a woman named Joice Heth, who he claimed was the one-hundred-sixty-one-year-old former nurse of George Washington. No stunt was too big or too outrageous for Phineas T. Barnum, not if it lured the people under his circus tent, gave them a thrill they would not soon forget, and made them remember his name.

For every outrageous, impossible, wonderful idea that Barnum imagined, for every magical moment under the bright lights of his circus tent, there were a thousand behind-the-scenes details and frequent logistical nightmares. These were left in the hands of James Bailey. He was the man who knew how to move a six-and-a-half-ton elephant from London to New York, who knew how to transport over twelve hundred performers, a menagerie of animals, and one hundred sixty-eight thousand yards of canvas across the country, and who knew that eight tons of promotional material, including fifty thousand posters, would ensure a successful one-hundred-night stand in London. Whatever Phineas Barnum could imagine, James Bailey could make happen.

Barnum and Bailey worked together for only slightly more than a decade before Barnum's death ended their alliance, but Barnum's passing did not end the revolution in American entertainment that the two had begun. Barnum and Bailey did not invent the circus. Ancient Greece and Rome had circuses, as did eighteenth-century England and colonial America. What Barnum and Bailey did was make the circus bigger and better and available to all Americans. Their paths crossed in an era when Americans seemed to have forgotten the value of good old-fashioned entertainment. With their spirit of showmanship and their continual striving for improvement and perfection, Barnum and Bailey gave the country something to marvel at, something to laugh at, something to talk about, and something to anticipate with great excitement. Thanks in great part to the brief friendship of Phineas Barnum and James Bailey, the circus has become a cherished tradition of American childhood and a permanent part of our national culture.

TRAVELER'S Diary

Tim Hamling

Detail of 1,000-square-foot scale model of P. T. Barnum's three-ring circus. Photograph courtesy of The Barnum Museum.

The Barnum Museum

In keeping with its founder's world-famous slogan, "the greatest show on earth," the Barnum Museum in Bridgeport, Connecticut, promises to celebrate its one hundredth birthday this year with "the greatest centennial ever." Special exhibits and year-round programs have been planned that would make P. T. Barnum, the legendary entertainer and showman, proud.

Prominently located in downtown Bridgeport, the Barnum Museum's unique exterior architecture has been fittingly described as "Barnumesque." The three-story building combines elements from the Romanesque, Byzantine, and Gothic styles. The first floor's red sandstone exterior gives way to columns, rounded arches, and intricately sculpted friezes as eye-catching as many of Barnum's famous attractions.

Inside, the museum's first floor salutes Barnum through a selection of his personal possessions and special displays. Family portraits and private treasures, including a library recreated from one of his estates, have been preserved to offer visitors a glimpse of Barnum's personal life. Eight individual installations focus on the varied roles that Barnum played in his life: businessman, civic leader, world-wide entertainer, and circus showman. A special highlight is a six-foot animated statue of Barnum that welcomes visitors to the museum with a recorded message.

An ornamented stairway leads to the museum's second floor, which contains exhibitions devoted to nineteenth-century Bridgeport and Barnum's involvement with the city. This preservation of Bridgeport's social history remains

44

The gallery of clowns. Photograph courtesy of The Barnum Museum.

true to the museum's original purpose of housing the Bridgeport Scientific Society and the Fairfield County Historical Society. A Victorian Picture Gallery celebrates the period's decorative arts through sculptures and period paintings, and a second gallery highlights Barnum's four Bridgeport mansions. Several mini-theaters showcase Bridgeport's nineteenth-century historical and industrial accomplishments through displays and recorded messages.

The Barnum Museum's third floor celebrates "Barnum: the Showman of the World." Sideshow banners reminiscent of the handbill advertisements that Barnum circulated to promote his exhibits hang from the walls. One gallery is devoted to Barnum's first two museums—the American Museum and the New American Museum—and the oddities that captivated and entertained so many visitors. The "Feejee Mermaid," a "two-headed" calf, an Egyptian mummy, and a Punch-and-Judy puppet show continue to amuse audiences today.

A special exhibit devoted to Barnum's legendary protégé, General Tom Thumb, recreates his Bridgeport home and displays many of his personal belongings, including furniture, clothing, and miniature carriages. The museum also salutes clowns, the mainstay of Barnum's circus, with a display of over-sized clothing, hammers, horns, instruments, and other props that have helped endear clowns to their audience.

For many, the museum's highlight is its one-thousand-square-foot scale model of Barnum's complete three-ring circus. Hand-carved acrobats, clowns, and animals perform for an enthusiastic audience under the Big Top. Every detail, from the circus wagons to the tent stakes, has been meticulously crafted in honor of P. T. Barnum's *Greatest Show on Earth*. Like the museum in which it is housed, this model celebrates and preserves Barnum's novel style of showmanship and entertainment.

The Barnum Museum, which was placed on the National Register of Historical Places in 1972, owes its own preservation to many people. It acted as a home for Bridgeport's local historical and scientific societies until the city took over the building in the 1930s and incorporated the museum with city hall. The museum's exhibits were allotted only a small space on the third floor. Interest in the building as a museum resurfaced in the 1960s; and, focusing on Bridgeport's history and the circus, it became the Barnum Museum in 1968. In 1986, civic and business organizations sponsored a major renovation to preserve the museum's treasures for future generations. Like the spirit of P. T. Barnum and his passion to entertain and amaze, the Barnum Museum is prepared to please audiences for another one hundred years.

COLLECTOR'S CORNER

Tim Hamling

AMERICAN HOMESTEAD AUTUMN by Currier & Ives, 1869.

The Lithographs of Currier & Ives

During the second half of the nineteenth century, the legendary printing tandem of Nathaniel Currier and James Ives produced thousands of lithographs reflecting all aspects of American life. For a public lacking television, illustrated magazines, and news photography, these mass-produced lithographs satisfied the curiosity aroused by events that could be read about but not always seen. Today, these prints have become a very popular collectible for an American public nostalgic for a simpler lifestyle.

Although the two printers are now men-tioned inseparably, Currier and Ives did not become partners until 1857, over twenty years after Currier had begun producing prints in 1835. Collectors, however, do not discriminate between prints bearing the "N. Currier" publishing line or the more famous "Currier & Ives" mark. Rather, they primarily seek prints according to their subject matter.

Hunting, fishing, farming, landscapes, cityscapes, horses, trains, steamboats, firemen, homes, and sports are just some of the scenes and events that Currier and Ives captured with their prints. In total, the team produced nearly seven

THE FARMER'S HOME—AUTUMN by Currier & Ives, 1864.

thousand different prints, an impressive number that testifies to their popularity. The thousands of original copies of each print that were produced have provided today's collectors with plenty of lithographs to pursue, so many that collections often concentrate on a single motif.

Original prints fit roughly into three sizes—small, medium, and large folios—and the value of a print generally increases in relation to its size. Smaller prints originally sold for as little as ten cents but are now bought and sold for hundreds of dollars. The larger prints, which originally sold for as much as four dollars, have been sold for more than ten thousand dollars, quite an accomplishment for pictures that Currier and Ives advertised as the "cheapest Ornaments in the World." The large-folio prints that depict nostalgic themes of home and family or uniquely American scenes of trains, steamboats, or even a baseball game, are currently the most sought by collectors.

Since they were produced for the general public, the prints are expected to show some evidence of handling and aging; tears, however, will decrease a print's value. Most collectors look for horizontal prints with enough of the original margin remaining around the design to be suitable for framing.

Carefully studying a print's color will help a collector distinguish between an original lithograph and a reproduction. The originals were hand-colored by artists who applied one color each and worked in assembly-line-like conditions. This hand-application produced soft, uneven colorings that could not be reproduced by modern techniques. Spending the time studying a print's colors can save a collector from paying an original's price for a contemporary reproduction.

The millions of contemporary reproductions that exist, however, do allow anyone to collect Currier and Ives prints. Collectors who simply enjoy the nostalgic scenes are just as happy owning the more affordable modern copies. Whether you seek original prints or reproductions, you, like so many others, can own a small piece of Americana.

FRIENDS THROUGH CORRESPONDENCE

Elsie M. Farr

I have found that friends who live
One thousand miles away
Have added color to my life
Through written words each day.

They always show more interest
Than friends along the street
Who do not know my thoughts at all
Though many times we meet.

I've found companionship so dear
Through looked-for envelopes
Containing inspiration of
My deepest dreams and hopes.

I would not trade this priceless gift
For anything on earth
Because through correspondence I
Have found what friends are worth.

Photo Opposite
DISTANT GREETINGS
Original Painting by Richard Hook

Attractive flowers and birds decorate a nineteenth-century calling card.

Getting in Touch Was Sometimes Tough

Anita Heistand

The whir of buggy wheels announced many callers to midwestern American farm homes in the 1800s. It would seem that the sound of the bouncing buggy, emphasized by barking dogs and nickering horses, might have made calling cards unnecessary; but the flowered favors, inscribed with a person's name, title, and street address, were widely used. Both townspeople and countryfolk depended on this transplanted old-world custom to announce social visits.

Sixteenth-century German students in Padua, Italy, are credited with originating the use of calling cards. Before returning to their homeland, the students called on their professors and left symbols of friendship in the form of miniature color drawings or a coat of arms below which the visitor wrote his name and the date. Several of these first tokens survive, the earliest dated 1560. By the eighteenth century, callers had begun to leave handwritten cards as a record of their unfruitful visits. Engraved cards appeared around 1750 and by 1770 were in common use in Milan and Rome.

Early calling cards were decorated with a garland of flowers surrounding the name; later, ornamental symbols appeared. Finally, whole scenes, landscapes, architectural monuments, or human figures covered the card so fully that very little space remained for a name.

In France, some visiting cards imitated playing cards; these displayed a person's name

Intricate script lettering adorned many calling cards.

across or between rows of hearts or other symbols taken from a deck of cards. French card styles became more sober when Louis XVI ascended the throne in 1774. In the late eighteenth century, Russian and German visitors to France and Italy used simple cards bordered by a conventional motif. In later years, lithographed cards became popular.

Favored on the midwestern farms of Nebraska, lithographed cards filled a real need for people whose homesteads were separated by acres of countryside. Paying a visit meant bringing the horses in from work or the pasture and grooming and equipping them to pull the buggy. Roads were so hard and bumpy when they were dry that

Callers often expressed personal sentiments on their cards.

they sent up clouds of dust and so soft when wet that the buggy wheels sank to their axles. Consequently, callers expended great effort to visit their neighbors and did not want their efforts to be fruitless.

Callers also had to be considerate of those they visited. Since many people worked hard and

Landscaped scenes added even more color to a calling card's design.

As calling cards became more elaborate, ornamental symbols were used to reflect a caller's personality.

did not always appreciate drop-in company catching them busy or dirty with their work, one afternoon a week was usually set aside for visiting and receiving guests. Calling cards became necessary as those who were visiting neighbors on this day were also being visited by other neighbors.

Sometimes a hired girl accepted calling cards from arriving guests before checking to see if the ladies of the family were ready to receive company. In a modest home where the family was present, no calling card was used; but if the family were absent, a tray would be waiting near the door to receive calling cards from visitors. Then, the family knew who deserved a return visit.

In the nineteenth century, ladies carried their calling cards in their reticules, and men tucked their cards into their vest pockets. During this period, calling cards reflected the personality of the giver, and both men and women used elaborately decorated cards. Designs varied from plain white cards with straight lettering to pastel cards with fancy script. More elaborate cards were lavishly colored with embossed layers that expressed a sentiment and lifted to reveal a name. These cards resembled today's greeting cards. The

dressiest calling cards were fringed with silk.

The caller's status could tactfully be revealed by the card's design. For example, a single gentleman might use cards featuring bachelor's button flowers. Some cards hid surprises—an apparently modest white rectangle with plain black lettering might, when held up to a light, become transparent and reveal a hidden scene. In the nineteenth century, calling cards made fashionable gifts, similar to stationery today.

Business people have continued to use a form of calling card with the business cards they carry. As busy and on-the-go as everyone is today, and as difficult as they are to reach by telephone, calling cards might become a drive-by, drop-in notice of remembrance again.

All photographs are from the collection of Anita Heistand, who collects calling cards at her home in Kansas.

Trimmed edges and an embossed surface marked the fanciest calling cards.

FELINE FRIENDS, Gay Bumgarner, Photographer.

That's What I Call a Friend

John Burroughs

One whose grip is a little tighter,
One whose smile is a little brighter,
One whose deeds are a little whiter,
   That's what I call a friend.

One who'll lend as quick as he'll borrow,
One who's the same today as tomorrow,
One who will share your joy and sorrow,
   That's what I call a friend.

One whose thoughts are a little cleaner,
One whose mind is a little keener,
One who avoids those things that are meaner,
 That's what I call a friend.

One, when you're gone, who'll miss you sadly,
One who'll welcome you back again gladly,
One who, though angered, will not speak madly,
 That's what I call a friend.

One who is always willing to aid you,
One whose advice has always paid you,
One who's defended when others flayed you,
 That's what I call a friend.

One who's been fine when life seemed rotten,
One whose ideals you have not forgotten,
One who has given you more than he's gotten,
 That's what I call a friend.

MAN'S BEST FRIEND, Gay Bumgarner, Photographer.

A SLICE OF LIFE

Edgar A. Guest

First Name Friends

Though some may yearn for titles great
    and seek the thrills of fame,
I do not care to have an extra
    handle to my name.
I am not hungry for the pomp of
    life's high dignities;
I do not sigh to sit among
    the honored LL.D.'s.
I shall be satisfied if I can
    be unto the end,
To those I know and live with here,
    a simple first-name friend.

There's nothing like the comradeship
    which warms the lives of those
Who make the glorious circle of
    the Jacks and Bills and Joes.
With all his majesty and power,
    old Caesar never knew
The joy of first-name fellowship
    as all the Eddies do.
Let them who will be "mistered" here
    and raised above the rest;
I hold a first-name greeting is
    by far the very best.

Acquaintance calls for dignity.
    You never really know
The man on whom the terms of pomp
    you feel you must bestow.
Professor William Joseph Wise
    may be your friend, but still
You are not certain of the fact
    till you can call him Bill.
Hearts grow warm, and lips grow kind,
    and all the shamming ends
When you are in the company of
    good old first-name friends.

The happiest men on earth are not
    the men of highest rank;
The joy belongs to George, and Jim,
    to Henry and to Frank;
With them the prejudice of race and
    creed and wealth depart,
And men are one in fellowship
    and always light of heart.
So I would live and laugh and love
    until my sun descends
And share the joyous comradeship
    of honest first-name friends.

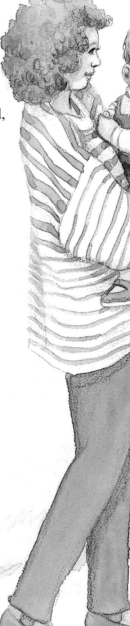

Edgar A. Guest began his illustrious career in 1895 at the age of fourteen when his work first appeared in the Detroit Free Press. *His column was syndicated in over 300 newspapers, and he became known as "The Poet of the People."*

Ann L. Cummings

Friends

Author Unknown

If nobody smiled and nobody cheered
And nobody helped us along;
If everybody looked after himself,
And good things all went to the strong;

If nobody cared just a little for you,
And nobody thought of me,
And we all stood alone in the battle of life,
What a dreary old world this would be!

Life is sweet just because of the friends we have made
And the things which in common we share;
We want to live on, not because of ourselves,
But because of the people who care.

It's giving and doing for somebody else;
On that all life's splendor depends.
And the joy of this world, when it's all added up,
Is found in the making of friends.

THROUGH MY WINDOW

Pamela Kennedy

Friends

Somewhere between their babyhood and late teens, an interesting transformation occurred in my relationships with my children. I'm not sure exactly how it happened, but my children have become my friends. The change took place subtly and in such a way that I was quite surprised the first time I acknowledged it.

Long ago, in the days of bottles, burps, and banging spoons, I recall saying to a friend, "Do you suppose these kids will ever grow up and be able to do anything for themselves?" It seems almost comical now, but deep into diapers, one loses perspective.

Then the "triumphant twos" came along—I prefer calling them that instead of the "terrible twos." They were certainly terrible at times, but there were those moments of glory when my little one stood before me wearing his clothes backward or clutching a paper covered with erratic crayon lines, announcing, "I did it myself!" There were so many firsts in the second year—first full-blown temper tantrum, first time to put the cat in the toilet, first broken bone!

When school started, I lost a lot of stature in my children's eyes. "Teacher" became the expert. I might have known everything the day before school started, but no longer. Of course, I could always be counted on to whip up a batch of cookies for the class party or fashion a Halloween costume at a moment's notice, but that was different. I had become the resource center around the house. "Mom, where's my dried frog?" "Have you seen my purple skirt?" "How could you throw out that moldy bread? It was my science fair project!"

I also served a vital role as Secretary of Transportation. I put thousands of miles on the trusty van hauling Cub Scouts, soccer teams, baseball teams, small ballerinas, large history projects, friends, enemies, and total strangers. It was expected. That's what Moms do.

All this is not meant to sound like a litany of complaints. There were lots of happy moments, but in all these roles, there was seldom time to be anything but a Mother—to be the one who passed out the band-aids, cookies, and answers, who picked up and dropped off on time and without comment.

When the adolescent years arrived, I was assigned an even more challenging task. It was understood that I should be as invisible as possible. In public, I was to remain particularly anonymous, never acting like I recognized my offspring. The only exception to this was in case of a purchase. At the mall, I could surreptitiously sidle up to the cash register, produce my credit card, and pay for a purchase as long as I didn't act like I knew my child was the customer. Conversations became more oblique and usually ended with exclamations: "How could you!" "Don't you get it?" "Are you serious?!"

Just recently I've noticed a change taking place. The other day, my son asked me out to breakfast! We took off on a frosty Saturday and ate at a local fast food restaurant—his treat! As we munched on our hash browns and scrambled eggs, we talked—really talked—about friends and ideas and dreams and frustrations. As we listened to one another, I began to realize we were developing a friendship.

Now, when my oldest child comes home from work, he often seeks me out. He'll plop his nearly six-foot frame in the rocker near my desk and engage in a bit of banter. There is a friendly camaraderie about our conversations. His observations of life are not nearly as one dimensional as I had thought, and I see him listening when I express an idea—not necessarily agreeing, but at least listening.

I've been thinking a lot about these changes lately, and I think kids are a little like the stock market. You begin by investing a little here and there, more and more as the years go by. There are times when it seems like the investment has gone bust; but then things level off again, and the value begins to climb. Then, one day, the dividends begin to roll in, and you can enjoy the fruit of your labor.

It has been great to have three children, but I suspect it will be even more rewarding to have three very wonderful friends!

Pamela Kennedy is a free-lance writer of short stories, articles, essays, and children's books. Wife of a naval officer and mother of three children, she has made her home on both U.S. coasts and in Hawaii and currently resides in Washington, D.C. She draws her material from her own experiences and memories, adding bits of her imagination to create a story or mood.

Handmade Heirloom

BASKET QUILT by Margaret Murray, Harpeth Clock and Quilt Company. Photograph by Robert Schwalb.

Quilting

Heidi King

Quilting is one of the very few crafts that create not only functional works of art, but friendships as well. Nowhere is this more evident than in history books and generations of family histories that describe in detail the happenings at early American community quilting bees. Most recollections depict a similar scene: children are turned loose to roam as they please while the women huddle around a half-finished quilt stretched across a heavy oak quilting frame as the aroma from the potluck supper waiting in the kitchen wafts from the open window on the porch and mingles with the whispers of gossip and heavy laughter that fill the air. While quilting techniques may have originated in Europe, American quilters can be credited with

turning the craft into a popular social pastime. As a result, a quilt was not only a combination of a variety of fabric scraps, but also the combined work of a variety of stitchers.

Ironically, today's heirloom quilts so carefully displayed or lovingly folded and stored for safe keeping were actually created out of the need to stay warm rather than the desire to decorate. In fact, the word *quilting* is derived from the Latin word *culcita*, which means "cushion" or "stuffed mattress." Examples of this type of art have been traced to pieces made as long ago as the first century, A.D., and the intricacy of these primitive pieces hints at an even earlier origin.

Around 1775, early Dutch and English settlers brought quilting to the American colonies, where it quickly flourished into the most famous American folk art. Understandably, times were hard for the settlers, supplies were limited, and social gatherings were one of the few means of entertainment. Quilting provided an answer to each of these hardships.

Initially, most quilts were worked without patterns, but as favorite designs increased in popularity, they received names such as Log Cabin, Star of Bethlehem, and Stars of Seven Sisters. In addition to being stitched for the sole purpose of warmth, the quilts also made excellent gifts. Wedding quilts were presented to newlyweds, and freedom quilts were given to young men at their coming of age. Even friendships were commemorated by a quilt with each block designed and signed by a different person.

There are two very distinct types of quilting. Wadded quilting is the earliest type and was used to provide warmth and protection. Wadded quilting is produced by sandwiching a layer of quilt batting between two layers of fabric and then stitching the three layers together. Primarily used for bed coverings and clothing, wadded quilting was usually stitched on white linen with patterns handed down from generation to generation. Romans used this type of quilting to make cushions, mattresses, and bed coverings; and soldiers wore quilted coats as protective covering.

The second form of quilting, which employs purely decorative stitching, includes both cord and trapunto quilting. These techniques became popular during the thirteenth century in Italy, although they had been previously in Persia, India, and Turkestan. Only two layers of fabric are used, and the patterns are often pictorial. In corded quilting, a cord is threaded through the channel between two lines of narrow stitching to form a type of raised design. In trapunto quilting, the pattern is emphasized by stuffing the design with a soft padding which also creates a raised effect.

Quilting goes hand-in-hand with two other closely related forms of needlework—patchwork and appliqué—and the three are often used together. Patchwork involves stitching scraps of fabric together to make a larger, more functional piece of fabric. For appliqué, patches are cut into shapes and attached to fabric by fancy stitching around the edges.

While the hardships that necessitated making quilts are past, many needleworkers still choose to express themselves through quilting, and even quilting bees are making a comeback within social circles. Although today's quilts are not made solely for functional purposes, their intricate patterns and stitching techniques still reflect the life and times of yesterday's crafters.

Heidi King makes her home in Tallahassee, Florida, and loves all arts and crafts.

To Autumn

John Keats

Season of mists and mellow fruitfulness,
Close bosom-friend of the maturing sun,
Conspiring with him how to load and bless
With fruit the vines that round the thatch-eaves run;
To bend with apples the moss'd cottage-trees,
And fill all fruit with ripeness to the core;
To swell the gourd, and plump the hazel shells
With a sweet kernel; to set budding more,
And still more, later flowers for the bees,
Until they think warm days will never cease,
For summer has o'er-brimmed their clammy cells.

Who hath not seen thee oft amid thy store?
Sometimes whoever seeks abroad may find
Thee sitting careless on a granary floor,

Thy hair soft-lifted by the winnowing wind;
Or on a half-reap'd furrow sound asleep,
Drows'd with the fume of poppies, while thy hook
Spares the next swath and all its twined flowers.
And sometimes like a gleaner thou dost keep
Steady thy laden head across a brook;
Or by a cider-press, with patient look,
Thou watchest the last oozings hours by hours.

Where are the songs of Spring? Ay, where are they?
Think not of them, thou hast thy music too,
While barred clouds bloom the soft-dying day
And touch the stubble-plains with rosy-hue;
Then in a wailful choir the small gnats mourn
Among the river sallows, borne aloft
Or sinking as the light wind lives or dies;
And full-grown lambs loud bleat from hilly bourn;
Hedge-crickets sing; and now with treble soft
The red-breast whistles from a garden-croft;
And gathering swallows twitter in the skies.

What Is Gold?

Stella Craft Tremble

The pumpkins store their food in bags of gold
Near Indian corn heaped by in tawny shocks;
A wedge of wild geese feel the crispy cold
While honking through the azure sky in broken flocks.

The topaz plumes of goldenrod in fields,
Where maples spill their coins along the fence,
Nod at full apple trees that flaunt their yield;
A wood thrush sings a song in recompense.

Persimmons scent the frosty, tangy air,
And autumn's gold is sprinkled everywhere.

Photo Opposite
FRUITS OF HARVEST
Norman Poole, Photographer

Ideals' Family Recipes

Favorite recipes from the *Ideals'* family of readers.

Editor's Note: If you would like us to consider your favorite recipe, please send a typed copy of the recipe along with your name and address to *Ideals* Magazine, ATTN: Recipes, P.O. Box 140300, Nashville, TN 37214-0300. We will pay $10 for each recipe used. Recipes cannot be returned.

CARAMEL POUND CAKE

Preheat oven to 275°. Grease and lightly flour a 10-inch tube pan and set aside. Combine 1½ cups of margarine, 1 box of light brown sugar (approximately 2¼ cups), packed, and 1 cup of granulated sugar; cream until light. Add 5 eggs, one at a time, beating after each addition. Combine 3 cups of flour with ½ teaspoon of baking powder, sifting to mix; stir into sugar-egg mixture. Slowly add 1 cup of milk and 1 teaspoon of maple flavoring, beating to mix well. Pour batter into prepared pan and bake for two hours or until a toothpick inserted into cake comes out clean. Cool cake in pan on rack for 10–15 minutes; turn out on plate and let cool thoroughly.

To glaze, in a large saucepan, combine ½ cup of margarine, 1 cup of dark brown sugar, packed, ¼ cup of milk, and 1 teaspoon of vanilla. Bring to a boil and boil without stirring 3–5 minutes to a soft-ball stage. Cool glaze to lukewarm, then drizzle over cake, letting glaze run down sides.

Jean Fuller Kistler
Candler, North Carolina

CHOCOLATE CANDY BAR CAKE

Preheat oven to 350°. Grease a 10-inch tube pan and set aside. In a mixing bowl, sift 2½ cups of flour, ½ teaspoon of baking soda, and ¼ teaspoon of salt; set

aside. In a second mixing bowl, cream 1 cup of margarine and 2 cups of sugar until light and fluffy. Add 4 eggs, one at a time, beating well after each addition. Stir in ¾ cup of chocolate syrup, mixing well. Add 1 cup of buttermilk alternately with the flour mixture, stirring after each addition. Over low heat, melt seven 1.55-ounce milk chocolate candy bars and add to mixture. Pour batter into prepared pan and bake for about 70 minutes. Remove pan from oven and let cake sit 1 hour in pan before removing.

Louise Higgins
Houston, Texas

FRESH CREAM CAKE

Preheat oven to 350°. Grease a 9x13-inch cake pan and set aside. In a bowl, sift together 2 cups of flour and 1 teaspoon of baking powder and set aside. Separate 4 eggs; slightly beat the egg yolks and set aside. With an electric mixer, beat the egg whites until stiff peaks form. Add beaten egg yolks, 1½ cups of heavy cream, and 1½ cups of sugar, beating after each addition until mixture is light and fluffy. With mixer on medium, gradually add flour mixture. Mix in the grated peel from 1 orange, ½ cup of chopped walnuts, and 1 teaspoon of vanilla.

Pour batter into prepared cake pan and bake for 35 minutes or until toothpick inserted in the middle comes out clean. Remove from oven and cool on a wire rack.

Neeharika William
Ratlam, India

Editor's Note: The following recipe makes an excellent topping for the fresh cream cake.

ORANGE GLAZE

In a saucepan, combine ¾ cups of sugar, ½ cup of sour cream, ½ cup of margarine, and 2 tablespoons of orange juice. Heat until butter is melted, stirring ingredients to mix. Bring to a boil and boil for 3 minutes while stirring continuously. Remove glaze from heat and, while glaze is still hot, use to coat cakes, rolls, or fresh breads. Glaze will thicken as it cools.

Judy Kneeland
Brentwood, Tennessee

Old Apple House in Autumn

Grace Noll Crowell

Seeping down the cracks in the knotted ceiling,
And lifting from the depths of the earthen floor,
An oddly released and subtle scent comes stealing
From the hoardings of many an autumn gone before.
And now afresh the Pippins, Baldwins and Russets
Heaped high in bushel baskets add their scent
To linger long in this ancient house long after
Their color is gone and their brief earth-life is spent.

Out of an orchard whose feet are ever wading
Ankle-deep in a glittering mountain stream
Have come the apples, crimson and green and golden,
As the bright fulfilment of some man's ancient dream
Of sturdy weighted trees whose abundant fruitage
Would gleam like lighted fires across the gloom
Of autumn days—waiting the inevitable hour
To be gathered close in the dusk of this mellow room.

50 YEARS AGO

Bringing in the Sheaves

I t's harvest time. The American farm, which takes its name from the early Anglo-Saxon word "fearme," meaning food, is yielding the fruits of the land again—food to fight for freedom.

Crops now being reaped cost long hours of toil, determined effort to compensate for labor and machinery shortages, and loss from flood and drought. Farmers battled against the elements,

70

and against time in their war on the food front. Figures indicate they won a gallant victory—four per cent more food produced than the all-time record last year!

Even as they bring in the sheaves, however, America's farmers are making plans to meet still greater needs in 1944—plans for food and fiber vitally important to winning the war and the peace to follow. Planting of 380,000,000 acres is the goal for next year, five per cent more than the 1943 harvested acreage. With nearly every crop a war crop, the farmer's aim for the new year will be to make the best use of as much acreage as he can plant.

He will try to top the all-time records set in 1943 for dry beans, dry peas, white potatoes, sweet potatoes, and flaxseed for oil. Greater emphasis will also be placed on cereals, including increased wheat acreage, and there will be special need for more soybeans, canning crops, and feed crops. Maintenance of the 1943 record level for all meats and for eggs, as well as keeping dairy products figures stepped up, will be another part of the job.

Record demands have been absorbing the farmer's record food production, and he has been asked for more. During seven consecutive years he has provided that "more" asked for each season. He expects to do it again in '44.

Printed in The Christian Science Monitor, *October 9, 1943.*

October's Bright Blue Weather

Helen Hunt Jackson

O suns and skies and clouds of June,
And flowers of June together,
Ye cannot rival for one hour
October's bright blue weather:

When loud the humblebee makes haste,
Belated, thriftless vagrant,
And goldenrod is dying fast,
And lanes with grapes are fragrant;

When gentians roll their fringes tight
To save them for the morning,
And chestnuts fall from satin burrs
Without a sound of warning;

When on the ground red apples lie
In piles like jewels shining,
And redder still on old stone walls
Are leaves of woodbine twining;

When all the lovely wayside things
Their white-winged seeds are sowing,
And in the fields, still green and fair,
Late aftermaths are growing;

When springs run low, and on the brooks,
In idle golden freighting,
Bright leaves sink noiseless in the hush
Of woods, for winter waiting;

When comrades seek sweet country haunts,
By twos and twos together,
And count like misers, hour by hour,
October's bright blue weather.

O suns and skies and flowers of June,
Count all your boasts together;
Love loveth best of all the year
October's bright blue weather.

Photo Opposite
FLAMING AUTUMN
Rutherfordton, North Carolina
Norman Poole, Photographer

AN AUTUMNAL TONIC

James Whitcomb Riley

What mystery is it?
      The morning as rare
As the Indian Summer may bring!

A tang in the frost and
      A spice in the air
That no city poet can sing!

The crimson and amber and
      Gold of the leaves
As they loosen and flutter and fall

In the path of the park, as it rustlingly weaves
Its way through the maples and under the eaves
 Of the sparrows that chatter and call.

What hint of delight is it tingles me through?
 What vague, indefinable joy?
What yearning for something divine that I knew
 When a wayward and wood-roving boy?

Ah-ha! and O-ho! but I have it, I say;
 Oh, the mystery brightens at last;
'Tis the longing and zest of the far, far away,
For a bountiful, old-fashioned dinner today
 With the hale harvest-hands of the past.

A Leaf-Treader

Robert Frost

I have been treading on leaves all day
  until I am autumn-tired.
God knows all the color and form of leaves
  I have trodden on and mired.
Perhaps I have put forth too much strength
  and been too fierce from fear.
I have safely trodden underfoot
  the leaves of another year.

All summer long they were over head,
  more lifted up than I.
To come to their final place in earth
  they had to pass me by.
All summer long I thought I heard them
  threatening under their breath.
And when they came it seemed with a will
  to carry me with them to death.

They spoke to the fugitive in my heart
  as if it were leaf to leaf.
They tapped at my eyelids and touched my lips
  with an invitation to grief.
But it was no reason I had to go
  because they had to go.
Now up my knee to keep on top of
  another year of snow.

Photo Opposite
FALLEN MAPLE LEAVES
Vernon County, Wisconsin
Darryl R. Beers, Photographer

UNTIL

Mary Jeannette Bassett

Until I have seen
    the last leaf fall
From the maple's crimson side,

Until I have seen
    on a copper sea
The full moon's beauty ride,

Until I have seen
    from the orchard grass
The young quail, startled, fly,

I cannot return to
  the streets of town
And a factory-lighted sky.

Until I have heard
  the blackbirds scold
In a sea-green field of grain,

Until I have heard
  the rising wind
And the quick reply of rain,

Until I have heard
  from the scarlet woods
The pheasant's evening call,

I cannot return to
  a barren town
And leave the wealth of fall.

Readers' Forum

Many years ago our girls' piano teacher let me read *Ideals* magazines while waiting during their lessons. I fell in love with their beauty and had to have a subscription.

I recently renewed my subscription again. I am so thankful you include poems by Edgar A. Guest in each issue. When I was ten years old, my parents gave me a little book of his poems, *Just Folks*, and I loved it. I kept it all these years and recently gave it to my ten-year-old granddaughter. I hope she will keep it and give it to her daughter someday.

Thanks for giving such enjoyment all these years in your beautiful, inspiring magazine.

Margaret Weideman
Walton, Kentucky

Editor's Note: Cleone Davis from Ocoee, Florida, submitted this picture of "Cinderella in her Pumpkin Shell," her five-month-old granddaughter, Angeleah Evans.

ideals®
Celebrating Life's Most Treasured Moments